THE
WELSH NARROW GAUGE
IN COLOUR

PETER JOHNSON

First published 1993

ISBN 0 7110 2126 0

© Ian Allan Ltd 1993

IAN ALLAN
Publishing

Terminal House   Shepperton TW17 8AS
Telephone: 0932 228950
Fax: 0932 247520   Telex: 929806 IALLAN G
Phototypesetting/printing: Ian Allan Printing Ltd at their works at
Coombelands in Runnymede, England

Front cover:
At Porthmadog, Festiniog Railway driver Colin
Dukes eases *Mountaineer's* regulator open to start
another journey across the Cob and through the Vale
of Ffestiniog to Blaenau Ffestiniog on 30 May 1992.

Above:
In November 1992 the Brecon Mountain Railway withdrew its steam mainstay, Jung 0-6-2T *Graf Schwerin-Löwitz*, from traffic requiring a new boiler. A fully booked series of Santa trains saw Vale of Rheidol Railway No 9 *Prince of Wales* transported from Aberystwyth to Pant at the end of November. The locomotive worked all services on the four pre-Christmas weekends and is seen on the last day, 20 December, leaving Pontsticill.

Previous page:
Immediately after leaving Welshpool, on the Welshpool & Llanfair Light Railway, the line climbs at 1 in 29 for nearly a mile, the steepest gradient on any preserved passenger railway, called the Golfa Bank. On 28 July one of the railway's original locomotives, *The Countess*, has no difficulty with the gradient.

Contents

Introduction   3

The Great Little Trains of Wales:
Bala Lake Railway   4
Brecon Mountain Railway   12
Festiniog Railway   16
Llanberis Lake Railway   26
Talyllyn Railway   29
Vale of Rheidol Railway   39
Welsh Highland Railway   47
Welshpool & Llanfair Railway   51
Locosheds and Workshops   59

Other Railways and Museums
Conwy Valley Railway Museum, Betws-y-Coed   61
Rhyl Marine Lake Miniature Railway   61
Corris Railway Society   62
Fairbourne & Barmouth Railway   64
Festiniog Railway Museum, Porthmadog   66
Narrow Gauge Railway Museum, Tywyn   66
Garden Festival Wales   67
Gloddfa Ganol, Blaenau Ffestiniog   67
Great Orme Tramway   68
Snowdon Mountain Railway   71
Teifi Valley Railway   76
New Construction   80

Introduction

Collectively the Welsh narrow gauge railways must be one of the most visited tourist attractions in the Principality, popular with the 'ordinary' public as well as with enthusiasts. Some of the latter, of course, will take their non-enthusiast families on Welsh holidays with the intention that the interests of both parties will be provided for. 'Come and ride on this train and admire the beautiful scenery' is the exhortation. The next bit, 'If you can see past my head and shoulders whilst I'm hanging out of the window watching the loco-motive' is almost never likely to be heard aloud.

That said, the Welsh narrow gauge lines do run through some spectacular scenery and they do have a lot of variety in motive power and rolling stock to attract both tourist and the enthusiast. The scenery encompasses the mountains of North and South Wales, lakes, rivers, waterfalls, valleys and tunnels. Railways range from the famous Festiniog, with its Fairlies, to the tiny Teifi, with a single steam engine, via the Talyllyn, the first preserved railway, the Welshpool & Llanfair, with its varied stock from around the world, and the unique Snowdon Mountain Railway. Lines have gauges which range from 15in to 3ft 6in. Gradients range from level to 1 in 29 for adhesion lines and go as steep as 1 in 5.5 on Snowdon. Heights achieved range from just above sea-level to just below 3,561ft, the latter, naturally, on Snowdon. Locomotives come in all shapes and sizes and no two are alike, even on the Vale of Rheidol which nominally has three the same. Carriages date from 1863 to 1991, both on the Festiniog, although when it comes to 'the oldest train in the World', I tend to support the Talyllyn claim, for in their vintage train nothing is newer than 1867 whilst the Festiniog's has vehicles as recent as 1872 and 1873! Truly there is something for everyone.

In 1985 and 1991 I had published two collections of photographs of the Welsh narrow gauge railways, in the publishers' 'Railway World Special' series, which told the railways' stories and allowed some of this variety to be illustrated. The use of colour in these albums was perforce limited, so it is a pleasure to be able to present this album of colour photographs showing, substantially, how the railways appear today, and to give some idea, perhaps, of why they do have such a wide appeal. The intention was to avoid including special events or one-off occurrences, to show the railways as they are on a day-to-day basis, but this was not always possible if the best coverage was to be achieved. Particularly in 1992, three lines were running locomotives in a state which which is not likely to be repeated in 1993 — the Talyllyn running No 4 in Corris Railway livery instead of standard lined green; the Welshpool & Llanfair Light Railway running ex-Sierra Leone No 85 in an incomplete new livery; and the Festiniog Railway operating *David Lloyd George* both unfinished and with a temporary black livery. A view of the Garden Festival Wales funicular is also included; whilst this opera-tion was restricted to 1992 the funicular did not achieve daily opera-tion and few pictures of it working are likely to be published.

The book is divided into four sections. Firstly, the lines that are marketed jointly as the 'Great Little Trains of Wales', mostly the larger railways; secondly, a collection of photographs of interiors of loco sheds and workshops, mainly a closed shop to members of the public; thirdly, the other operating railways and a selection of rail-way museums, with no attempt made to achieve complete coverage; and lastly the construction of the Festiniog Railway's new locomo-tive, *David Lloyd George*. Unless stated otherwise all the pho-tographs were taken in 1992.

Some notes, now, for the photographically minded: prior to 1992 my photographs were taken using Olympus OM2n and OM2sp cam-era bodies, usually with a Zuiko 50mm f1.4 lens. From 1992 I have used a Nikon F601 body with a Nikkor 50mm f1.4 lens, supple-mented by Sigma 28mm f1.8 and 75-300mm f4.5-5.6 APO lenses. The built-in camera-top flash on the Nikon was used on most of the interiors and, except for a roll of Kodachrome 64 used on 20/1 August 1992, Kodachrome 200 film was used throughout.

I would like to express my sincere thanks to all the railways, their managements and personnel, for making these photographs possible. At each the welcome was unstinting and permission to go behind the scenes or off limits readily given.

To the reader, however, a caveat is necessary — the lineside pho-tographs were either taken from outside the railways' boundaries or by arrangement, with permission; their publication here is not an invitation to trespass. All photographs were taken by the author unless otherwise stated.

Peter Johnson
Leicester   December 1992

Of related interest, by the same author:

Portrait of the Festiniog; Ian Allan, 1992
Railway World Special: The Welsh Narrow Gauge Railways;
    Ian Allan, 1991

The Great Little Trains of Wales:

Bala Lake Railway

Above:
The Bala Lake Railway runs alongside the lake of that name, on the formation of the former Great Western Railway branch from Ruabon to Barmouth Junction (Morfa Mawddach) via Dolgellau. The main terminal of the 2ft gauge tourist line is at Llanuwchllyn, at the opposite end of the lake to Bala. One of the line's two Hunslets, *Holy War*, is seen at the water tank at Llanuwchllyn. The two Hunslets were originally built for the Penrhyn Slate Quarries in 1902 and 1903.

Above:
Visiting locomotive *Lilla* shunting bogie Hudson wagons loaded with coal at Llanuwchllyn on 5 September. *Lilla* is also a Hunslet, although larger than the line's resident *Holy War* or *Maid Marian*, and also spent its working life at the Penrhyn Slate Quarry.

Above:
Holy War simmers gently in the station at Llanuwchllyn on 29 July. The ex-Great Western line from Barmouth to Ruabon, via Bala, was closed on 18 January 1965.

Above:
Seen at Llanuwchllyn on 5 September, *Maid Marian* prepares to depart on its 4½-mile journey to Bala. The stretch of line from Llanuwchllyn to Pentrepiod was the first part of the narrow gauge line to open, on 14 August 1972, some seven years after the last BR train had operated.

Above:
The railway's second ex-Penrhyn Quarry Railway locomotive *Maid Marian* and train is seen passing behind Llangower church, close to Llangower station limits, on 5 September. Earlier in the year plaques had been affixed to the locomotive recording 25 years of ownership by the *Maid Marian* Locomotive Association.

Right:
Holy War heads east along the south bank of Bala Lake on 29 July. This locomotive was acquired in 1975 and, after restoration, entered service in 1979.

Above:
Almost at journey's end, *Holy War* makes a colourful scene as it nears Bala station on 29 July.

Right:
Having run round its train at Bala — the actual station is beyond the bridge — *Holy War* prepares to return to Llanuwchllyn.

Brecon Mountain Railway

Above:
The two foot gauge Brecon Mountain Railway presently occupies two miles of former Brecon & Merthyr Railway trackbed between Pant and Pontsticill, amidst the spectacular countryside of the Brecon Beacons. Pant is the major terminal, with an impressive station and workshops' building specially built, situated just off the Heads of the Valleys road north of Merthyr Tydfil. The train was photographed close to Pant on 26 May.

Above:

An impressive collection of locomotives has been collected for use on the Brecon Mountain Railway, much of it obtained from overseas. The line's regular steam locomotive came from what used to be East Germany and is an Arn Jung 0-6-2WT called *Graf Schwerin Löwitz*. In prospect for the fairly near future is a South African 2-6-2+2-6-2T Garratt, the restoration of which is approaching completion. *Graf Schwerin Löwitz* was photographed whilst running round at Pontsticill on 24 May. Behind are two Vale of Rheidol Railway open tourist cars which have been overhauled on the BMR.

13

Graf Schwerin Löwitz leaving Pontsticill on 24 May. Behind the train can be seen Tal Fechan reservoir, stretching towards Brecon. The caboose was built, as was all the railway's passenger stock, in the line's own workshops; and is equipped to carry wheelchair-bound passengers.

On 24 May *Graf Schwerin Löwitz* heads away from Pant with a passenger service for Pontsticill on 24 May. Although the Brecon Mountain Railway is only 1¼ miles long at this stage, long term plans envisage reopening the line north from Pontsticill to Torpantau— a distance of 3¾ miles.

15

Festiniog Railway

Above:

The Festiniog Railway, which runs between Porthmadog and Blaenau Ffestiniog, was opened in 1836 to carry slate from the quarries at the latter to the wharves at the former. Following a period of closure from 1946 it was re-opened in 1955, becoming the second railway, after the Talyllyn, to be operated with volunteer support.

This line-up of locomotives, arranged especially for this book, was photographed at Porthmadog on 5 September. From the left are *Prince*, *David Lloyd George*, *Merddin Emrys*, *Mountaineer* and *Linda*, the last three being in steam. Linda was about to take the 09.45 departure to Blaenau Ffestiniog; *Mountaineer* and *Merddin Emrys* would later haul the 10.45 and 11.45 departures respectively.

Right:

Prince, built by George England in Hatcham, London, in 1863, is reckoned to be the oldest steam locomotive in regular use in the World. Driver Mick Whittle is seen checking that the locomotive has been uncoupled before running round at Minffordd when operating the Porthmadog-Minffordd shuttle on 29 August.

Left:
David Lloyd George is the latest Boston-Lodge built double Fairlie to enter traffic on the Festiniog Railway, first hauling passenger trains, in an incomplete condition, on 21 July. The locomotive is seen with a

Down train nearing Minffordd Cemetery on 31 August with the summit of Snowdon visible behind.

Above:
Mountaineer was built by the American Locomotives Co for use in France during the World War 1. It came to the Festiniog Railway in 1967 and was captured leaving Penrhyn on 29 August.

Above:
Linda was built by Hunslet for the Penrhyn Quarry Railway in 1893 and has been at work on the FR since 1962. On 30 August it worked an evening train for members of the railway's Parks & Gardens Dept and is seen at Tan-y-bwlch during the refreshment stop.

Right:
A vintage shuttle train hauled by *Prince* leaving Minffordd to return to Porthmadog on 29 August. The newest vehicle in the train is the green bogie brake/3rd composite, No 10, which dates from 1873.

Above:
Diesel *Upnor Castle* is not commonly seen on passenger trains but was captured on the return 'Early Bird' (08.45 ex Porthmadog) on 31 August, when it was climbing between the two level crossings at Tanygrisiau.

Right:
Faithfully restored to its Victorian condition prior to its re-entry into service in April 1988, 'Double-Fairlie' *Merddin Emrys* makes an impressive sight on 31 August outside Boston Lodge Works. The locomotive dated originally from 1879 and was one of two similar locomotives built at Boston Lodge at the end of the 19th century.

Left:
Heading past Boston Lodge Works before crossing the Traeth Mawr Embankment, *Conway Castle*, rebuilt in the mid-1980s, hauls a passenger service towards Porthmadog on 31 August. This locomotive was repainted in 1990 following the installation of equipment for push-pull operation.

Above:
Festiniog Railway 2-4-0STT *Linda* crosses the Traeth Mawr Embankment on Saturday 17 August 1991 with the 13.30 Porthmadog-Blaenau Ffestiniog. The 1893-built Hunslet is seen in the lined blue livery in which it was repainted during the previous winter. The embankment — commonly known as

The Cob — was originally built in 1811 and was utilised for the railway when the line was built in the 1830s. *Andrew Fox*

Llanberis Lake Railway

Above:
The Llanberis Lake Railway is a 2ft gauge line which runs alongside Llyn Padarn using two miles of the old 4ft gauge Padarn Railway trackbed. The railway's major terminal, and only public access, is at Gilfach Ddu, in the Padarn Country Park at Llanberis.

On 14 June the Railway's three Quarry Hunslets are seen outside Gilfach Ddu depot being steamed for the Llanberis Transport Festival. From the front they are *Thomas Bach* (formerly *Wild Aster*), *Elidir* and *Dolbadarn*.

Right:
At Gilfach Ddu *Dolbadarn* waits to leave with a passenger train, with the wagon train alongside, on 14 June. This 0-4-ST was built by Hunslet in 1922.

Above:
During the Transport Festival a rake of slate wagons and a gunpowder van was borrowed from the Welsh Slate Centre at Gilfach Ddu and given a run out along the Lake Railway. *Elidir* provided the haulage and is seen here entering the loop at Cei Llydan, the railway's halfway point and the location of a picnic area.

Talyllyn Railway

Above:

In 1950 the Talyllyn Railway became the first preserved railway in the world. It had survived since 1865 with its original locomotives and rolling stock and with most of its original rail. In 1950 it was not in a good condition. With the advent of the preservationists all that has changed; additional locomotives and rolling stock have made an appearance to run on relaid and extended track and the original stock overhauled and in regular service. The 2ft 3in gauge railway starts at the coastal resort of Tywyn and runs 7½ miles inland to Nant Gwernol, three quarters of a mile beyond Abergynolwyn station, the original passenger station.

Nos 1 *Talyllyn* and 2 *Dolgoch* and the original rolling stock are seen returning to Tywyn at Brynglas on 26 September; the station is just visible in the trees and the block post which controls a passing loop, to the left, is behind the locomotives.

Above:
A close-up of No 1 *Talyllyn* standing at Tywyn Wharf station waiting to take the 15.15 train up to Nant Gwernol on 21 August.

Right:
No 2 *Dolgoch* pilots No 1 *Talyllyn* at Forestry Crossing, Abergynolwyn, on 26 September; No 2 is painted in the livery it carried in 1950.

Left:
No 3 *Edward Thomas* was also originally a Corris Railway locomotive and in November 1991 received Corris livery temporarily. This repainting was initially intended to last seven days. However, following a protracted winter overhaul it was returned to service in time for use during the peak timetable operation in 1992, still in the temporary livery. The photograph was taken at Abergynolwyn on 21 August; driver, but firing on this occasion, David Jones prepares to hand the Quarry Siding-Abergynolwyn single line token to the signalman as the train comes to a stand.

Above:
No 6 *Douglas* at Forestry Crossing, between Abergynolwyn and Nant Gwernol on 26 June. The next day was the locomotive's last in passenger service before withdrawal for a major overhaul, including replacement of its original 1918 boiler.

Above:
In 1991 the Talyllyn Railway joined the exclusive ranks of the locomotive builders, when No 7 *Tom Rolt* entered traffic. Built at Pendre Works incorporating components from a Barclay locomotive built for the Irish Peat Board, No 7 was named after the leader of the Talyllyn preservation movement. The locomotive was seen with a Tywyn-Nant Gwernol non-stop working at Brynglas crossing on 26 September.

Right:
With the driver keeping a watchful eye on the photographer, No 6 *Douglas* approaches Nant Gwernol on 26 June its penultimate day of public operation before being withdrawn for a major overhaul. *Douglas* was built by Barclays in 1918.

Far left:
No 1 *Talyllyn*, built by Fletcher Jennings in 1865, takes water at Dolgoch on 21 August whilst *en route* for Nant Gwernol.

Left:
No 6 *Douglas* steams gently on its way back to Tywyn on 26 June. The 7½-mile route from Tywyn to Nant Gwernol was opened gradually from 1951 onwards, with the final stretch, from Abergynolwyn being completed in 1976.

Right:
The Talyllyn's terminus in Tywyn is but a short walk from the British Rail station on the Cambrian Coast route. The close proximity is a reflection of Talyllyn's history — it was designed to bring slate from the quarries at Bryn Eglwys down to the main line for onward shipment. No 6 *Douglas* awaits departure from Tywyn on 26 June.

Vale of Rheidol Railway

Above:
The Vale of Rheidol Railway achieved fame as the last steam railway operated by British Rail. It is a 2ft gauge line 11½ miles long, starting from the main line station at Aberystwyth and running up to Devil's Bridge. Since privatisation in 1989, when the line was taken on by the owners of the Brecon Mountain Railway, a major investment programme has been implemented, affecting most parts of the railway.

The locomotive overhaul programme commenced in the winter of 1989/90, when No 9 *Prince of Wales* travelled to the Brecon Mountain Railway's workshops to return with a higher cab, air braking and a new maroon livery. It is seen, with the village of Llanbadarn Fawr behind, on 20 August.

Above:
No 9 runs past the Vale of Rheidol locomotive shed, with No 7 *Owain Glyndŵr* standing outside, returning to Aberystwyth with the last train of the day on 20 August. The shed was built for standard gauge locomotives and converted for narrow gauge purposes by British Rail in 1968. The difference in the cab heights of the two locomotives is detectable in this view.

Right:
No 9 crossing the newly rebuilt timber bridge over the Afon Rheidol on 20 August. This is a popular spot for local people, usually children, to play and sunbathe.

Left:
With the driver sounding the whistle for the level crossing, No 7 approaches Nantyronen station, where water will be taken, on 21 August. Gravel is extracted from the far bank of the river.

Below:
In 1982 No 9 was specially repainted into its original Vale of Rheidol livery. As the locomotives were unnamed under Cambrian ownership, No 9 was therefore to be seen for a short period without its nameplates but when photographed on Sunday 13 August 1983 the locomotive had regained its *Prince of Wales* plates. It is seen here on a working towards Devil's Bridge. Subsequently, the locomotive has been repainted and has lost this attractive colour scheme. *Andrew Fox*

Above:
No 7 'in the car park' at Devil's Bridge on
20 August.

Above:
The cab interior of No 7 whilst pounding up the steep grade to Devil's Bridge on 20 August. The dial on the right is for the recently installed air braking system.

Right:
No 7, with Shaun McMahon still at the controls, arrives at the intermediate station of Aberffryd with a train *en route* to Devil's Bridge on 21 August. The Vale of Rheidol, some 11¼ miles in length, climbs 680ft between Aberystwyth and Devil's Bridge, of which 480ft is achieved in four miles over the 1 in 50 gradient from Aberffryd and Devil's Bridge.

Above:

In the early 1980s, the Vale of Rheidol was one of the few parts of British Rail to escape from the corporate 'Rail Blue'. No 9 *Prince of Wales* was repainted in the original company's livery in 1982 and in the following year the line's coaching stock was turned out in Great Western chocolate and cream. No 9 makes a spectacular and colourful sight as it hauls a rake of chocolate and cream coaches across the original timber viaduct at Afon Rheidol in 1983.

46

Welsh Highland Railway

Above:
The Welsh Highland Railway runs a line three quarters of a mile long on the former standard gauge Beddgelert Exchange Siding at Porthmadog. The railway is ambitious to obtain access to the original Welsh Highland Railway trackbed.

The railway has several steam locomotives which were built in Britain and which were exported. *Karen*, seen here at Porthmadog on 31 May, was obtained from Rhodesia. It was originally manufactured by Peckett in 1942.

Left:
Karen waits outside the Welsh Highland's shed at Gelert's Farm on 31 May.

Above:
The only surviving steam locomotive to survive from the original Welsh Highland Railway is *Russell*. Built by Hunslet in 1906 it is seen here at Porthmadog being prepared for its next duty.
David W. Allan

Welshpool & Llanfair Light Railway

Left:
The Welshpool & Llanfair Light Railway is another narrow gauge railway which survived to be operated by British Railways, carrying coal and cattle and not being closed until 1956. 2ft 6in gauge, it runs for 8½ miles from the outskirts Welshpool to Llanfair Caereinion, more or less parallel to the Dolgellau road.

No 2 *The Countess* simmers at the western terminus of Llanfair Caereinion on 28 July.

Above:
Under the watchful eye of one of the train crew, *The Countess* gingerly approaches its rake of coaches at Llanfair Caereinion on 28 July. The coaching stock of the Welshpool & Llanfair Light Railway includes a number of British-built coaches repatriated from Sierra Leone, in Africa, as well as several from Austria.

Far left:
Seen in 1984, No 10 *Sir Drefaldwyn* was built by
Franco-Belge in 1944. This 0-8-0T was built in
France to a German design for use by the German
forces and was acquired from the Steiermarkische
Landesbahnen in Austria during 1969.

Left:
Immediately after leaving Welshpool the line climbs
at 1 in 29 for nearly a mile, the steepest gradient on
any preserved passenger railway, called the Golfa
Bank. On 28 July one of the railway's original locomotives, *The Countess*, makes an impressive sight
as it ascends the bank. Welshpool & Llanfair
services to Welshpool were restored in 1981 to a
station on the outskirts of the town; the original link
through the town to the British Rail station was last
used in the early 1960s and is now abandoned.

Right:
One of the more back-breaking jobs on any pre-served railway is the loading of coal. Here No 2 *The Countess* is seen being coaled on 28 July. *The Countess*, and companion *The Earl*, were both built by Beyer Peacock and delivered to the line in 1902 in time for the line's opening in 1903. Operated by the Cambrian Railways, the line passed to the Great Western at Grouping in 1923 and the two locomotives became Nos 822 and 823. These numbers were retained by British Railways after Nationalisation in 1948 through to the line's closure in 1956.

Far right:
A little bit of Africa in deepest Wales; Sierra Leone No 85, a Hunslet-built 2-6-2T dating from 1954, hauls a rake of coaches from Sierra Leone during the summer of 1987.

Above:
The Countess crosses an ungated level crossing near Castle Caereinion on 28 July.

Right:
Set amongst the attractive countryside of Mid Wales, the Welshpool & Llanfair has grown substantially since the first preservationists moved onto the line in 1962. The first section was reopened in April 1963 and for 30 years the line has provided one of the most popular tourist sites in the area. Seen in verdant countryside *The Countess* gently passes the photographer on 28 July.

Above:
The station buildings at Welshpool (Raven Square) were opened in 1992, the main one, on the left, being transported from Herefordshire; here they provide a backdrop for *The Countess* running round its train, which includes a British-built bogie coach obtained from Sierra Leone, on 28 July.

Loco Sheds and Workshops

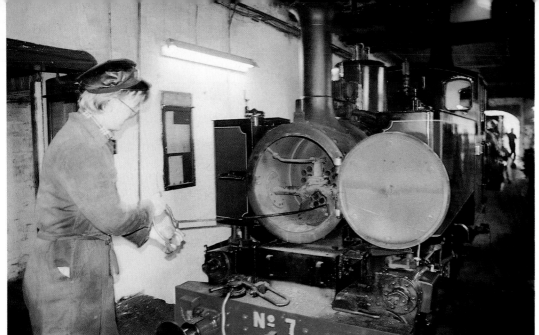

Left:
No 7 *Tom Rolt* undergoing tube cleaning in Pendre loco shed, Talyllyn Railway, on 22 August.

Left:
The Snowdon Mountain Railway's workshops at Llanberis seen on 1 September with a number of the Swiss-built 0-4-2Ts under repair. In the foreground can be seen two sets of the geared driving wheels which provide traction over the steeply graded line.

Right:
Vale of Rheidol No 7, *Owain Glyndŵr*, is pictured in pristine BR lined Brunswick Green livery on 19 June 1983 prior to its recommissioning. The Vale of Rheidol's shed at Aberystwyth was originally designed for use with standard gauge locomotives and only become the narrow gauge locomotives' home in 1968.

Right:
Resplendent in its red livery, *Prince* awaits its next turn of duty in Boston Lodge Works in August. *Prince* was one of two locomotives supplied by George England in 1863 — the first to be operated by the Festiniog. Sister locomotive *Princess* has been displayed in the Harbour Station Museum since April 1981. *Britomart*, a 'Hunslet' 0-4-0T from Pen-yr-Orsedd Slate Quarry, faces the photographer.

Other Railways and Museums:

Conwy Valley Railway Museum, Betws-y-Coed

Left:
The Conwy Valley Railway Museum is to be found in the former goods yard of Betws-y-Coed station. Inside there are a number of dioramas and displays, including a 15in gauge scale model of 4-6-2 70000 *Britannia*. In the grounds there is an extensive 7¼in gauge railway and a short 15in gauge electric tramway, both shown here on 14 June.

Rhyl Marine Lake Miniature Railway

Left:
The Rhyl Marine Lake Miniature Railway is a circular 15in line designed by the famous miniature-railway engineer, Henry Greenly. The railway operates daily during July and August, weather permitting, with steam operation on Sundays, Mondays and Thursdays. One of the Barnes-built locomotives designed for the line by Greenly is seen in action on 18 August 1991.

Corris Railway Society

Above:
The Corris Railway Society has established a museum devoted to the Corris Railway in the railway's former stable block in the centre of Corris. In addition to several photographic displays, the museum contains several large exhibits.

The Corris Railway Society also has ambitions to rebuild part of the Corris Railway south of Corris and has already laid track between Corris and Maespoeth, the site of the former Corris locomotive shed, which is also in Society ownership. This photograph of a works train, taken on 26 June, gives some idea of the views to be had when the Society succeeds in its aims.

Above:
A view of the Corris Railway Society's Maespoeth Depot on 26 June with No 5 *Alan Meaden* hauling a works train. The Corris Railway had its origins as a 2ft 3in gauge mineral tramway opened in 1859. Passenger services were operated from 1883 through to 1930, when the Great Western took over. The final freight services were withdrawn in 1948 and the line was dismantled thereafter. The replica Corris Railway passenger coach is also in view.

Fairbourne & Barmouth Railway

Above:
The two-mile long Fairbourne & Barmouth Railway has a track gauge of 12¼in and uses half-size reproductions of famous narrow gauge prototypes as motive power. The railway starts across the road

from the Cambrian Coast Railway station at the small seaside resort of Fairbourne and runs onto sand dunes on the Mawddach estuary opposite the larger seaside resort of Barmouth. A connection is made across the river using small motor boats. The reproduction Lynton & Barnstaple Railway locomotive, *Yeo*, at Penrhyn Point on 15 August 1989.

Right:
At Penrhyn Point, the Fairbourne & Barmouth Railway constructed an artificial tunnel in 1984 at the same time as the line was reconstructed from 15in gauge to 12¼. This was the line's third gauge — it had originally been built as a two-foot horse tramway in the 1890s. The reproduction Lynton & Barnstaple locomotive *Yeo* emerges from the tunnel in August 1987.

Festiniog Railway Museum, Porthmadog

Right:
The Festiniog Railway Museum is located in the former goods shed at Porthmadog Harbour station. Major exhibits are *Princess*, the hearse van, now available for operational service, and two different slate wagons, one loaded with slate, and a diorama of Harbour station in the 1950s. The two former exhibits were captured on film on 29 August.

Narrow Gauge Railway Museum, Tywyn

Right:
The Narrow Gauge Railway Museum is located at the Talyllyn Railway's Wharf station. The exhibits relate to narrow gauge railways in general, as applied to the slate industry and the Talyllyn Railway in particular. Two of the seven locomotives displayed are shown in this 22 August photograph. The larger is No 2, a Kerr Stuart 0-4-0WT dating from 1902; the other is *Pet*, 18in gauge locomotives built by the London & North Western Railway and on loan from the National Railway Museum.

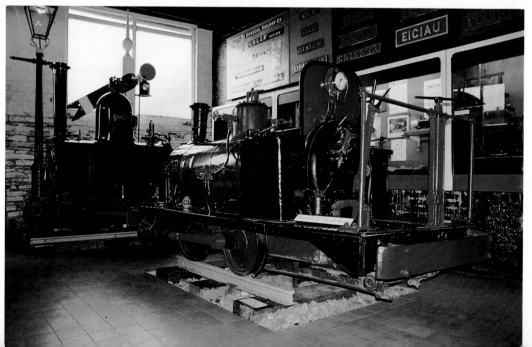

Garden Festival Wales

Right:
Garden Festival Wales was held at Ebbw Vale in 1992. A 900ft 3ft gauge funicular, installed on the hillside site for the duration of the show, was single track with a passing loop in the middle. The photograph shows one of the three-car trains ascending the lower section on 26 May. The winding gear was situated at the bottom station.

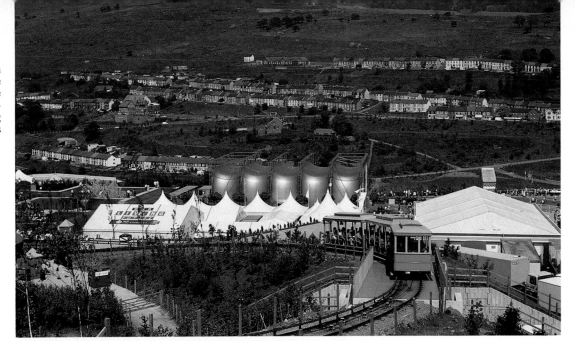

Gloddfa Ganol, Blaenau Ffestiniog

Right:
Gloddfa Ganol is a slate quarrying museum situated in part of the former Oakeley slate quarry at Blaenau Ffestiniog. The site also contains a large collection of narrow gauge railway exhibits, mainly internal combustion and un-restored. A 2ft gauge railway carries visitors from the shop to the mine entrance and is shown in action on 17 August 1989.

Great Orme Tramway

Left:
The Great Orme Tramway is a 3ft 6in gauge cable hauled system split into two parts, each about half a mile long; the lower section opened in 1902, the upper in 1903. The lower section runs through or alongside the public highway; on 1 September car No 5 is seen descending Old Road. Above and to the right of the tramcar can be seen one of the traffic lights at Black Gate, the only traffic control on the system.

Above:
On the upper section the tramway runs through the open countryside of the Great Orme Country Park. Also on 1 September, car No 7 is seen ascending the cutting as it approaches the summit. Car No 6 is on the left, heading for Halfway station, visible above car No 7.

Car No 5 descends the lower section and has just been signalled to cross the junction at Black Gate on 1 September. The four trams, which operate the two sections, were built by Hurst Nelson in 1902-03.

Snowdon Mountain Railway

The Snowdon Mountain
Railway is Britain's only
railway built in the manner
of the Swiss mountain railways, even to the extent of
having the metric gauge of
800mm. For most passen-
gers, a journey on the
$4\frac{1}{2}$ mile line starts at Llanberis, at the foot of the
mountain. No 8 *Eryri* and
its carriage are seen just
below Hebron on 1 Septem-
ber.

Left:
Hebron is the site of a passing loop, now fully automated with electricity obtained from a wind powered generator. The diesel-powered train was photographed on 1 September. Llyn Padarn is visible behind the station building and Llanberis Lake Railway trains are visible from this location.

Above:
Snowdon Mountain Railway steam locomotives take water at Halfway station, as seen here on 20 August 1991 with No 4 Snowdon being the beneficiary of the supply.

Above:
Clogwyn station viewed from a Down train on 20 August 1991. According to the weather trains sometimes terminate at Clogwyn; indeed, the track above gets filled with snow and ice each winter and every spring it has to be cleared by hand and the track refurbished before trains can return to the summit.

Right:
A dramatic view of No 4 *Snowdon* at Clogwyn looking down the mountain with Llyn Padarn in the distance on 20 August 1991. No 4 is one of eight locomotives supplied to the line by Schweierische Locomotiv-und Maschinenfabrik of Winterthur in Switzerland between 1895 and 1923.

Teifi Valley Railway

Left:
The Teifi Valley Railway is a 2ft gauge railway constructed on the trackbed of the former GWR Newcastle Emlyn branch, having a line about a mile long running westwards from its base at Henllan, north of Carmarthen. The line's sole steam locomotive, *Alan George*, is seen approaching Pontprenshitw when returning to Henllan on 25 May. *Alan George* was built for the Penrhyn Quarries and is one of the few not to have had a cab fitted in preservation.

Above:
The Teifi Valley Railway is unable to use the former standard (and broad) gauge station at Henllan as it is on a gradient; however, a line to the stock shed is laid through the old station site, seen here with diesel locomotive *Sammy* and the railway's coaching stock before services started on 25 May.

Left:
Alan George is seen at Henllan on 25 May. The ex-Great Western branch line from Newcastle Emlyn to Pencader closed to passenger services as long ago as 15 September 1952, but it (and the main Aberystwyth-Camarthen line) remained open for freight services until 1975. The construction of the narrow gauge line on part of the trackbed started in 1978 and the first services were operated in 1985.

Above:
The scene at Henllan on 25 May with *Alan George* and a rake of coaches in a livery derived from the traditional Great Western chocolate and cream. Although the running line of the Teifi Railway is only some 1,800yd long at the moment, ambitious plans envisage extensions both eastwards and westwards to give a total length of six miles.

New Construction

Right:

The Festiniog Railway has many claims to fame, not least the construction of its own double Fairlie locomotives. On 21 July *David Lloyd George*, still incomplete, hauled its first passenger train, double-headed with Linda in case of problems. The duo are shown leaving Tan-y-bwlch on that momentous occasion.

Below:

The late John Williams working inside the smoke-box of *David Lloyd George* with a gas torch on 31 May; the superstructure had been mounted on *Earl of Merioneth's* power bogies, the latter having been withdrawn for a boiler overhaul.

Back cover:

On 26 May 1992 the Brecon Mountain Railway's *Graf Schwerin Löwitz* heads towards Pontsticill, the valley of the Tal Fechan behind.